Bobby and Mandee's
Don't Hide
Abuse

by Robert Kahn

Illustrated by MaryAnn Barbetti

All marketing and publishing rights guaranteed to and reserved by

FUTURE HORIZONS INC.

721 W. Abram Street
Arlington, Texas 76013
800-489-0727
817-277-0727
817-277-2270 (fax)
E-mail: info@FHautism.com
www.FHautism.com

Illustrated by MaryAnn Barbetti

ISBN 13: 978-1-935274-53-7

PP, Logan, IA
6/11, 374730

DEDICATION
I wish to thank my family and friends for all of their
support with this book.

Robert Kahn

Hello Mandee, how was your day at school?

Bobby, it was fine, but I have a question for you. When you promise a friend that you will keep a secret, should you always keep that promise?

Well Mandee, that depends. If it is a secret like they still sleep with their teddy bear, then yes, you should keep your promise.

But if it is a secret that involves their safety, NO! There are stories about this, let me tell you one.

Brandon told his best friend, Zach, a secret. Brandon explained that his stepfather was abusing him. Mandee, the word, "abuse," means to misuse something. Brandon's stepfather was hurting him every night by hitting him.

Brandon made Zach promise not to tell anyone.
Zach kept his promise, because he didn't want
Brandon to be mad at him.

ABCDEFGHIJKLMNOPQRSTUVWXYZ

A few days later, Zach's teacher informed the class that she had terrible news to tell them.

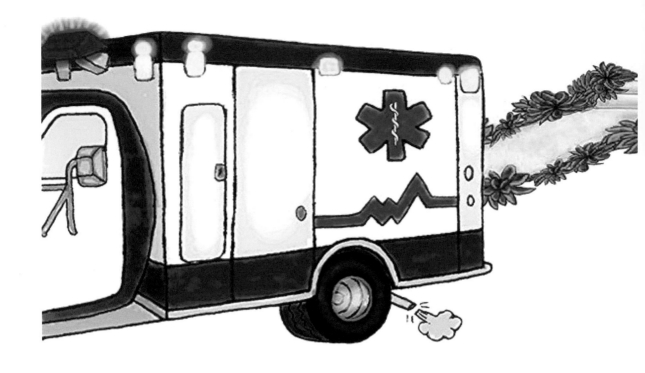

Brandon had been killed last night by his stepfather. He was taken to the hospital after his stepfather had beaten him, but it was too late.

The teacher then explained that if she had known this was happening to Brandon, he would still be alive.

ABCDEFGHIJKLMNOPQRSTUVWXYZ

principal   vice principal
secretary   teachers
counselor   lunch people
family
friends

She also explained that Brandon could have told anyone at school. This includes the principal, vice principal, counselor, secretary, duty and lunch people, maintenance, or any of the teachers.

These people are trained to believe children,
like Brandon, the first time they tell their story.

They would have told other people who would have protected Brandon from this abuse, and made sure he was safe.

How do you think Zach feels? He kept the secret, just as Brandon had asked. He had promised. He thought that if he told, Brandon would be mad at him and might not be his friend anymore.

Which is better, having a friend mad at you or having a friend seriously hurt or even dead? That's right Mandee, it's better to have them mad at you.

Since I heard that story, I asked Dad what children should do when they are in this situation.

He explained that, if a child is being abused,
he or she should try to get out of the house.

If they can't leave, they should use the phone at their own house and call 9-1-1.

If they can't use the phone, they should try to go somewhere safe. That is somewhere in the house where the abusive person isn't. They should stay there until the abusive person calms down.

As soon as the child can, he or she should
leave the house and go tell a trusted adult.

Sometimes, this will be the next day when the child goes to school.

Remember, a child can tell any adult that works at the school.

If it happens to be the weekend, then as soon
as possible tell a trusted adult. Again, this may
be the next day. If the adult they tell doesn't
believe the story, the child needs to keep talking
to trusted adults until he or she finds one who
will help them.

Thanks Bobby, this is what is happening to my friend, Aloha. Aloha has a big bruise on her stomach that I noticed. I asked her what happened.

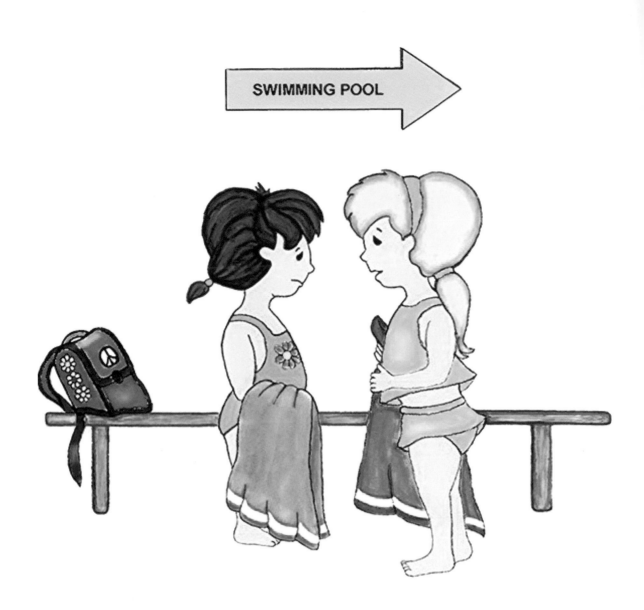

SWIMMING POOL

Aloha explained that sometimes her mother drinks too much beer. Then her mother's mood changes from a loving mom to a mean and hateful person. It's during this time her mother doesn't have any patience and Aloha gets kicked, punched, or hit.

Her mom always tells Aloha it is her fault because she did something wrong. Many times she tells Aloha that this is why she has to drink beer.

Then later, her mom is always really sorry and apologizes. She promises Aloha that it will never happen again. Unfortunately, her mother doesn't keep this promise and a few days later, it happens again.

Then, once more, her mother apologizes and promises that it will never happen again. But a few days later it happens. Each time this happens, Aloha gets beat worse and hurt more.

Mandee, it's not Aloha's fault! Abusive people make up reasons for what they do. That way they always have someone else to blame and it's never their own fault.

Come on, Mandee. For Aloha's safety, you can't keep this a secret. We have to tell Dad. He'll know what to do.

Bobby and Mandee's Abuse Test

1.   Is it a good idea to keep a secret if a child's safety is involved?

   (answer on page 4)

2.   What does the word, "abuse," mean?

   (answer on page 5)

3.   Who are trusted adults a child can tell that they are being abused?

   (answer on page 9)

4.   What should children do if they are at home and being abused?

   (answers on pages 15, 16, 17, 18, 19 and 20)

5.   Who can they telephone for help?

   (answer on page 15)

6.   If the child tells an adult and the adult doesn't believe them, what should the child do?

   (answer on page 20)

7.   When the abusive person apologizes, and promises they will never hurt the child again, do they keep this promise?

   (answers on pages 24 and 25)

8.   Is it the child's fault if they are being abused?

   (answer on page 26)

911 Tips for Parents

1.　Teach your children how to dial 911. A call to 911 should always be a call for help. A call to 911 from a pay pone is free.

Do your children know when to call 911?
- If there is someone injured or sick.
- If there is smoke or flames in the house.
- If they are home alone and someone is trying to get in.
- If a stranger follows them home from school.
- If they see a car accident.
- If they observe someone being hurt by another person.
- If during a storm, they see a power pole or another object struck by lightning.

Do your children know when NOT to call 911?
- Never call 911 as a joke!
- Never call 911 just for information.
- Never call 911 just to see if it works!

2.　Be sure to stress the following two points with your child:

- NEVER get into a car with someone unless your parents know you're going with that person.
- ALWAYS tell your parents where you're going.

Other Important Information:
Children need to know their address, phone number, and the type of emergency help they need.

Address_____

Phone_____

Police_____

Fire_____

Medical_____

My List of Safe Grown-ups to Call

Name   Phone Number

_____   _____

_____   _____

_____   _____

_____   _____

_____   _____

_____   _____

_____   _____

_____   _____

_____   _____